Uranus

Lori Dittmer

seedlings

CREATIVE EDUCATION
CREATIVE PAPERBACKS

Published by Creative Education and Creative Paperbacks
P.O. Box 227, Mankato, Minnesota 56002
Creative Education and Creative Paperbacks
are imprints of The Creative Company
www.thecreativecompany.us

Design by Ellen Huber; production by Joe Kahnke
Art direction by Rita Marshall
Printed in the United States of America

Photographs by Art Resource (Bildagentur/Kupferstichkabinett,
Staatliche Museen, Berlin, Germany/Jörg P. Anders/Art Resource,
NY), Corbis (NASA), Creative Commons Wikimedia (NASA/JPL),
iStockphoto (aydinmutlu), NASA (NASA/JPL, NASA/JPL-Caltech),
Science Source (Mark Garlick, Gary Hincks, Shigemi Numazawa/
Atlas Photo Bank, Victor Habbick Visions), Shutterstock (NASA
images, Vadim Sadovski, janez volmajer), SuperStock (Science
Photo Library)

Library of Congress Cataloging-in-Publication Data
Names: Dittmer, Lori, author.
Title: Uranus / Lori Dittmer.
Series: Seedlings.
Includes bibliographical references and index.
Summary: A kindergarten-level introduction to the planet
Uranus, covering its orbital process, its moons, and such
defining features as its sets of rings, gases, and name.
Identifiers: ISBN 978-1-60818-919-9 (hardcover) / ISBN 978-1-
62832-535-5 (pbk) / ISBN 978-1-56660-971-5 (eBook)
This title has been submitted for CIP
processing under LCCN 2017938983.

CCSS: RI.K.1, 2, 3, 4, 5, 6, 7;
RI.1.1, 2, 3, 4, 5, 6, 7; RF.K.1, 3; RF.1.1

First Edition HC 9 8 7 6 5 4 3 2 1
First Edition PBK 9 8 7 6 5 4 3 2 1

TABLE OF CONTENTS

Hello, Uranus!

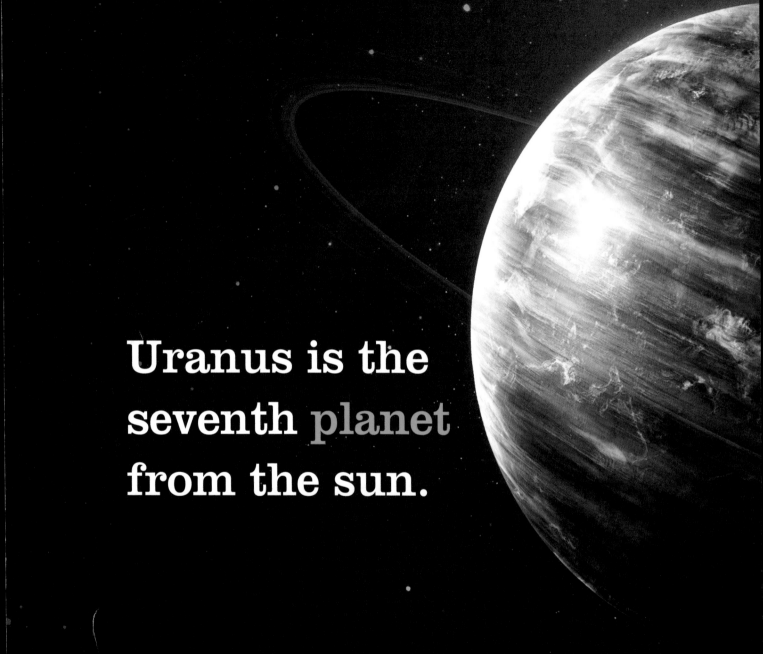

Uranus is the seventh planet from the sun.

Blue-green Uranus is cold. Most of it is made of gas.

Two sets of rings circle Uranus. The inside rings are dark. The outside rings look bright red and blue. There are 13 in all.

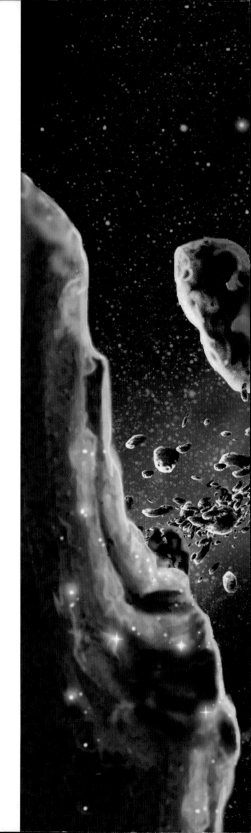

Many moons go around Uranus.

So far, 27 have been found! They are named after characters in books. The two largest moons are Titania and Oberon.

Uranus is four times wider than Earth. It takes the planet 84 years to orbit the sun.

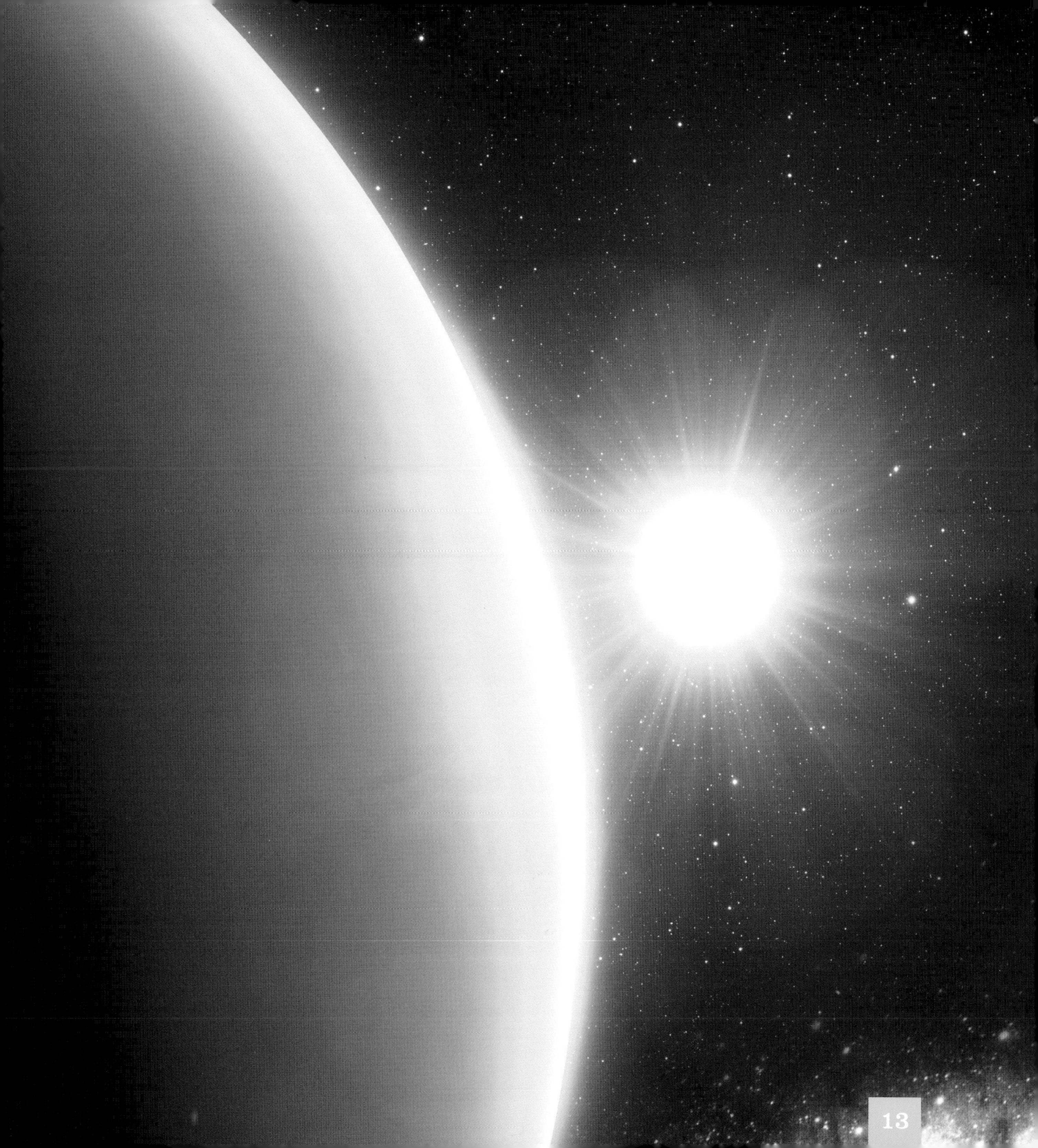

Astronomers study planets.

14

They found Uranus in 1781. It is named for an old story about the god of the sky.

Uranus spins on its side. Winds blow clouds.

Goodbye, Uranus!

Titania

rings

atmosphere

clouds

Oberon

21

Words to Know

characters: people in a story

god: a being thought to have special powers and control over the world

orbit: the path a planet, moon, or other object takes around something else in outer space

planet: a rounded object that moves around a star

Read More

Heos, Bridget. *Do You Really Want to Visit Uranus?*
Mankato, Minn.: Amicus, 2014.

Loewen, Nancy. *The Sideways Planet: Uranus.*
Minneapolis: Picture Window Books, 2008.

Websites

NASA Jet Propulsion Laboratory: Kids
http://www.jpl.nasa.gov/kids/
Build a spacecraft or play a planetary game.

National Geographic Kids: Mission to Uranus
http://kids.nationalgeographic.com/explore/space/mission
-to-uranus/#uranus-planet.jpg
Learn how Uranus moves through our solar system.

Index

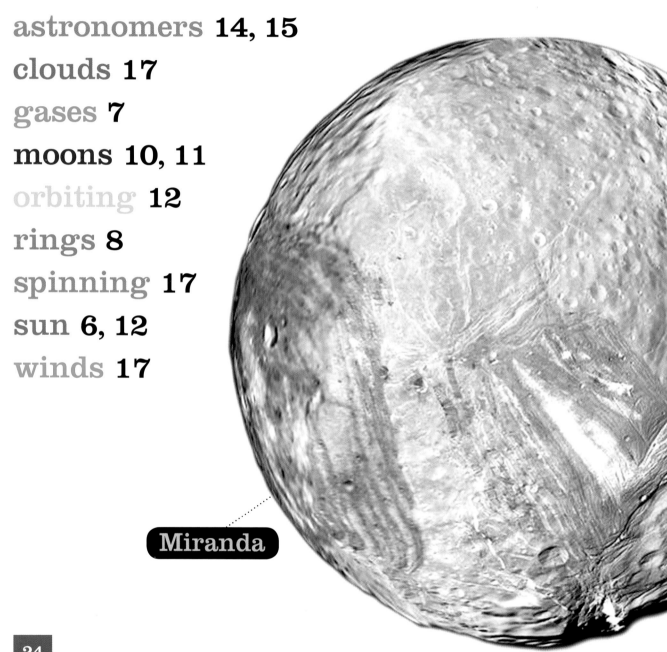

Miranda